PYRAMIDS

Anne Millard

Kingfisher

NEW YORK

KINGFISHER
Larousse Kingfisher Chambers Inc.
95 Madison Avenue
New York, New York 10016

First edition 1996
10 9 8 7 6 5 4 3 2

LIBRARY OF CONGRESS
CATALOGING-IN-PUBLICATION DATA
Millard, Anne,
Pyramids / Anne Millard—1st Amer. ed.
   p.   cm
Includes index.
Summary: Describes the pyramids of
Egypt and the Americas and their signif-
icance in the social, political, and
religious life of long-vanished civi-
lizations.
1. Pyramids—Egypt—Juvenile
literature. [1. Pyramids—
Egypt. 2. Pyramids. 3. Egypt—
Antiquities.] I. Title
DT 63.M516   1996
932--dc20
95-39660 CIP AC

ISBN 1-85697-674-2 (HC)
ISBN 0-7534-5051-8 (PB)

Author: Anne Millard
Consultants: George Hart,
Amanda Podony
Editor: Molly Perham
Design: John Jamieson
Typeset by Karin Ambrose
and Tracey McNerney
Art editor: Valerie Wright
Picture research:
Su Alexander
Printed in Spain

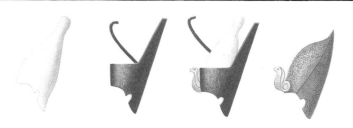

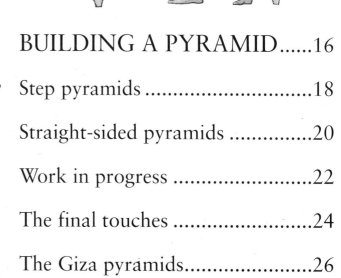

CONTENTS

THE PYRAMID AGE

Egypt is a very old country. It became a united nation about 5,000 years ago and for 3,000 years was ruled by its own kings. Egyptian history is divided into several periods. The three greatest were the Old, Middle, and New Kingdoms. During the Old Kingdom the Egyptian rulers built great stone tombs called pyramids. So, this period is also known as the Pyramid Age.

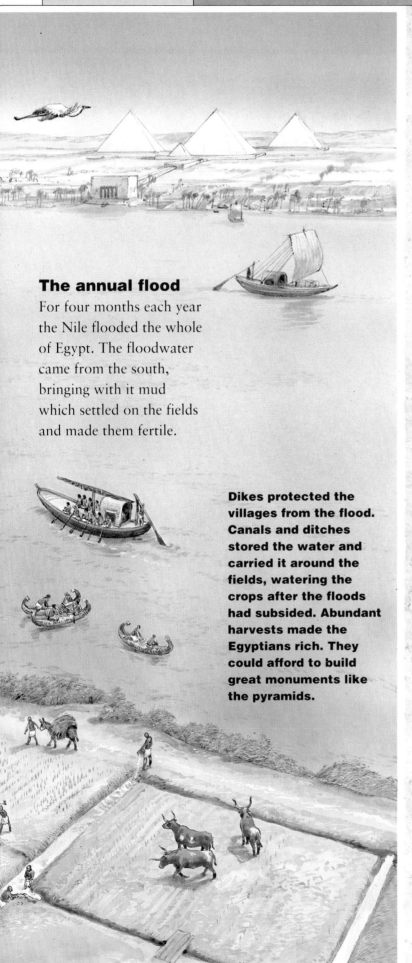

The annual flood

For four months each year the Nile flooded the whole of Egypt. The floodwater came from the south, bringing with it mud which settled on the fields and made them fertile.

Dikes protected the villages from the flood. Canals and ditches stored the water and carried it around the fields, watering the crops after the floods had subsided. Abundant harvests made the Egyptians rich. They could afford to build great monuments like the pyramids.

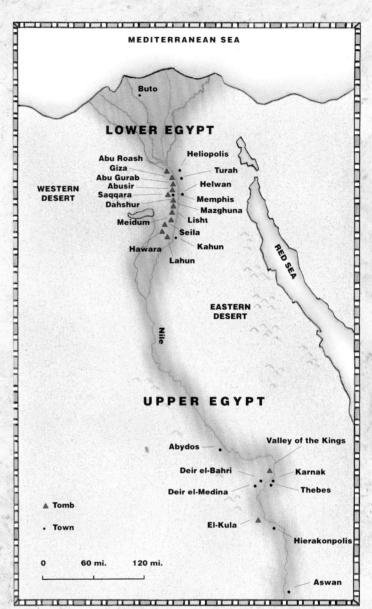

To the ancient Egyptians, the three most important things were their king, the Next World, and the Nile River. Egypt is a very dry country where it hardly ever rains. The Nile provides water for plants, animals, and people. The royal pyramids, which housed the body and possessions of dead kings, were built on the west bank of the Nile.

The king

Egypt was two separate kingdoms before it was united. The Egyptians never forgot this, and their ruler's title was King of Upper and Lower Egypt. The people knew that their king was very special. He was descended from Ra, the sun god. Also, when the king sat on the throne wearing all his regalia, the spirit of the great god Horus entered him and he spoke as god on earth.

▲ In carvings and paintings, the king was often shown twice, as King of Upper Egypt and King of Lower Egypt.

▲ When a new king took the throne, he ordered an architect to start work on his tomb immediately.

 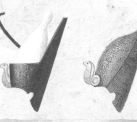

As god on earth, a king was revered in death as much as in life. His body had to be preserved, the goods he needed in the Next World had to be guarded against robbers, and his divine spirit had to be launched to join the gods in heaven. For all this, a very special monument was required—a pyramid.

▶ **The crook and flail were the king's symbols of authority.**

Choosing a site
The Land of the Dead was in the west, where the sun sets. So, for the king's tomb, a level site was chosen in the Western Desert. The work would take many years.

The people

Egypt's royal families are divided into dynasties. The Old Kingdom was ruled by Dynasties III to VI. Below the royal family were courtiers, high-ranking civil servants, generals, and high priests. Then came scribes, government officials, priests and priestesses, doctors, engineers, and soldiers. The fourth tier included craft workers, professional mourners, dancers, and servants. The majority were peasants and laborers.

◄ We can imagine ancient Egyptian society as if it were arranged in tiers, like a pyramid. At the top was the king. Only later kings were called pharaoh.

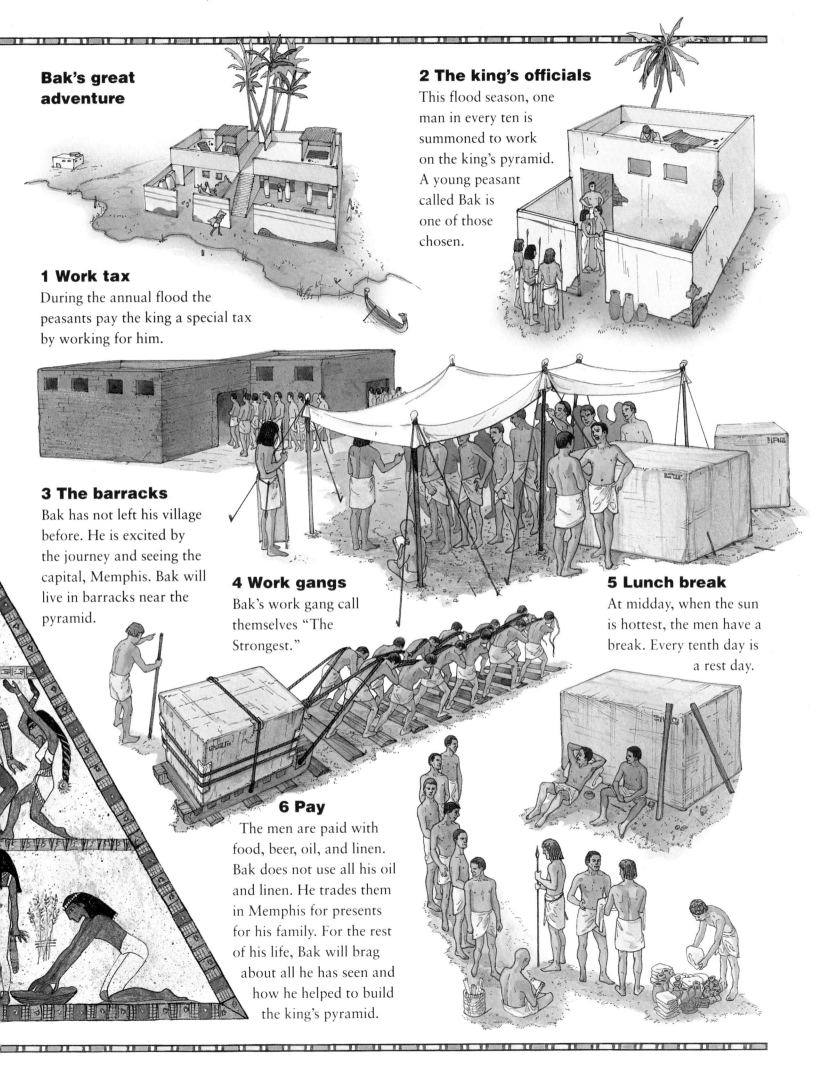

Bak's great adventure

1 Work tax
During the annual flood the peasants pay the king a special tax by working for him.

2 The king's officials
This flood season, one man in every ten is summoned to work on the king's pyramid. A young peasant called Bak is one of those chosen.

3 The barracks
Bak has not left his village before. He is excited by the journey and seeing the capital, Memphis. Bak will live in barracks near the pyramid.

4 Work gangs
Bak's work gang call themselves "The Strongest."

5 Lunch break
At midday, when the sun is hottest, the men have a break. Every tenth day is a rest day.

6 Pay
The men are paid with food, beer, oil, and linen. Bak does not use all his oil and linen. He trades them in Memphis for presents for his family. For the rest of his life, Bak will brag about all he has seen and how he helped to build the king's pyramid.

9

Craft workers and scribes

While the laborers hauled the huge blocks of stone, the more skillful work on the pyramid was done by trained craft workers. The workforce included surveyors, metalworkers, stonemasons, and carpenters. Painters and sculptors decorated the walls of the temples. Scribes kept records of all the materials needed.

▶ Written orders have been sent to the overseer of this limestone quarry to cut stone for the king's pyramid. Each block weighs nearly three tons. The men use ropes and levers to move them.

▶ A shallow trench is cut, outlining a block. Wooden wedges are driven in with a mallet. The wedges are then soaked with water. As the wood swells, the stone breaks away.

Metalworkers

Early Egyptians learned how to use copper and gold. They made tools, weapons, and beautiful jewelry. Later they discovered how to make the harder bronze from copper and tin by heating the ore in a furnace. By the time of the New Kingdom the Egyptians had invented bellows that were worked by foot. The molten metal was poured into molds. Metal tools were very valuable. The overseers issued them to the workers each day, and recorded their return.

◄ The quarry workers use ropes and levers to move the stone blocks. They will be stored until the time of the annual flood, when they will be loaded onto barges and rowed across the river to the building site.

▼ The blocks are roughly squared with a chisel and mallet and marked for later identification.

Scribes

A scribe sat cross-legged with a board across his knees. He wrote with a reed pen on paper made from papyrus reeds. His palette contained ink cakes and pens. Scribes were vitally important, but few families could afford the long education needed to learn the hundreds of hieroglyphs, or word pictures, that were used in writing.

Transportation

 The vast quantities of stone needed to build a pyramid were transported from the quarries by ship. During the annual flood the stones could be floated right up to the edge of the desert. Large ships for use on the Nile or at sea were built

with timber from Lebanon. Besides trading goods within Egypt, the Egyptians traded with eastern

▲ This held the ship's mast in place.

Mediterranean lands, Nubia, and Punt, to the south. Profits from trade helped to pay for pyramid building.

Land transportation

Small things were carried in baskets or yokes on the shoulders. Bulky goods such as grain were transported on donkeys. The horse arrived just before the start of the New Kingdom. Camels were not used until the Late Period.

▲ For crossing the Nile, ordinary Egyptians might use boats made of reeds. Noblemen used reed boats for fishing, fowling, and hunting hippopotamuses and crocodiles.

▼ On land, heavy items like stone blocks for the pyramids were put on wooden sledges and dragged along by teams of men or oxen.

▲ Egyptian ships were steered by one or two large steering oars that were fixed to the stern. The Egyptians were the first people to use sails.

Finding true north
A pyramid had to be aligned with the North Star, Polaris. Standing in the center of an enclosure, a priest noted the position of a star as it rose above the wall. He then waited and noted the position where it set below the wall. By bisecting the angle between him and the points of the star's rising and setting, the priest found true north.

Priests and gods

 The Egyptians worshiped dozens of different gods and goddesses. During their long history, some gained in popularity, while others fell from favor. The king headed all their cults, but in practice he appointed priests to act for him.

▲ Horus, the sky god, whose spirit entered the king. His eyes were the sun and moon.

▲ Ptah, the creator god, invented the arts. He was the local god of the capital, Memphis.

Since the earliest times, the Egyptian priests studied the stars. The movements of the stars, planets, and sun were the basis of the Egyptian calendar. They also used the stars to fix the exact position of the sides of a pyramid, which always faced the four compass points exactly.

▲ This Egyptian zodiac was carved on the ceiling of a shrine dedicated to Osiris in the temple of Dendera. It is now in the Louvre in Paris.

The foundation ceremony

The king and a priestess dressed as the goddess Seshat marked an outline with wooden posts linked by ropes. This ceremony was carried out in later times for the foundation of temples, and may also have been used for pyramids.

▲ Hathor, the goddess of love and beauty, once raised the sun up to heaven on her horns.

▲ Isis, sister and wife of Osiris, was the mother of Horus. She was a perfect wife and mother.

▲ Ra-Horakhty, the sun god and Horus joined together, is shown with the sun on a hawk's head.

▲ Osiris was the god of the dead. In his realm in the West, souls were judged and sentenced.

► The workers were housed in barracks. Skilled stonemasons and some laborers worked on the pyramid all year long, but thousands of people doing their work tax were brought in every flood season.

◄ A path of wooden rollers was made so that the sledges carrying the great stone blocks could be moved more easily. Full sledges went up one side of the ramp, empty ones came down the other side.

◄ Toiling under the hot desert sun was thirsty work. A constant supply of drinking water was needed for the laborers.

BUILDING A PYRAMID

Building a pyramid was a magnificent feat of organization and engineering. A large pyramid could take over twenty years to complete. The blocks were laid in layers, one layer at a time. They were dragged up a ramp made of bricks and rubble. As each layer was completed, the ramp was made higher and longer. Finally a casing of fine-quality limestone was put in place.

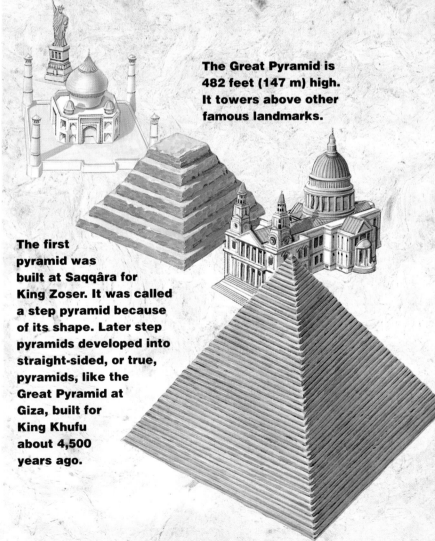

The Great Pyramid is 482 feet (147 m) high. It towers above other famous landmarks.

The first pyramid was built at Saqqâra for King Zoser. It was called a step pyramid because of its shape. Later step pyramids developed into straight-sided, or true, pyramids, like the Great Pyramid at Giza, built for King Khufu about 4,500 years ago.

Step pyramids

Zoser's architect, Imhotep, built the king's tomb in stone instead of mud brick. Then he put more stone steps on top, making the first pyramid. Why did he do this? The kings believed that their souls would join the Imperishable Ones—the northern stars that never set below the horizon. A step pyramid may therefore have been a symbolic stairway to the stars.

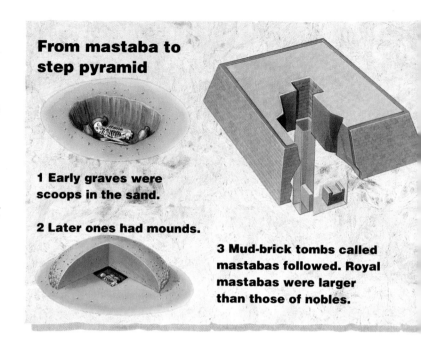

From mastaba to step pyramid

1 Early graves were scoops in the sand.

2 Later ones had mounds.

3 Mud-brick tombs called mastabas followed. Royal mastabas were larger than those of nobles.

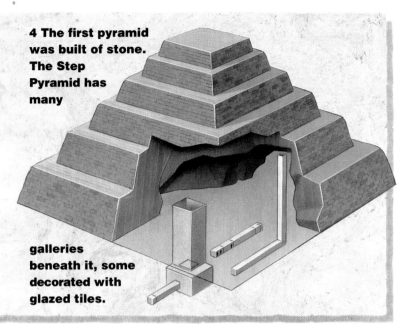

4 The first pyramid was built of stone. The Step Pyramid has many galleries beneath it, some decorated with glazed tiles.

First true pyramid

Huni built a step pyramid at Meidum. His son Sneferu turned it into a straight-sided pyramid, but the new casing came crashing down—bringing much of the original step pyramid with it. Was there a flaw in the design or in the building?

Zoser's pyramid is set in an enclosure with open courts and many buildings. The complex probably represents the palace and its offices. The other buildings are solid. But, by magic, the king could use them in the Next World.

A bent pyramid

Sneferu began a straight-sided pyramid at Dahshur. Halfway up, the engineers panicked. They thought the angle of the sides was too steep, so they changed it to a more gentle slope and created the Bent Pyramid.

The *heb sed* festival

When a king had reigned for thirty years he celebrated the magical *heb sed*. This festival was supposed to renew the king's strength. The ceremonies included a special run that symbolized taking control of his realm and also showed that he was physically fit.

Straight-sided pyramids

From Dynasty IV, all pyramids were built with straight sides. Religious writings called the Pyramid Texts promise the king that sunbeams would be strengthened so that he could walk up them to join Ra. Straight-sided pyramids may symbolize these ramps of sunbeams.

▲ Carvings on Mortuary Temple walls show us what Egyptian ships looked like.

spiral ramp

long straight ramp

The ramp

The Egyptians did not have cranes. To build a pyramid, they erected a huge ramp and dragged stone blocks up on sledges. Some historians have suggested that the ramp went around the pyramid from bottom to top. But the remains of ramps at unfinished buildings show that a single straight ramp was used. The Egyptians were prepared to build ramps as long and tall as necessary.

1 The Valley Temple

When a king died, his body was rowed across the Nile to the Valley Temple to be mummified.

2 The Causeway

A covered processional way led from the Valley Temple to the pyramid. The inside walls were often decorated, and holes in the roof provided light.

3 The Mortuary Temple

Built against the side of the pyramid, the Mortuary Temple was the place where priests made offerings to the king's spirit every day for eternity.

4 The queen's pyramid

A king would build a small pyramid for his queen.

5 The tomb

The king and all his belongings were buried in a chamber beneath the pyramid.

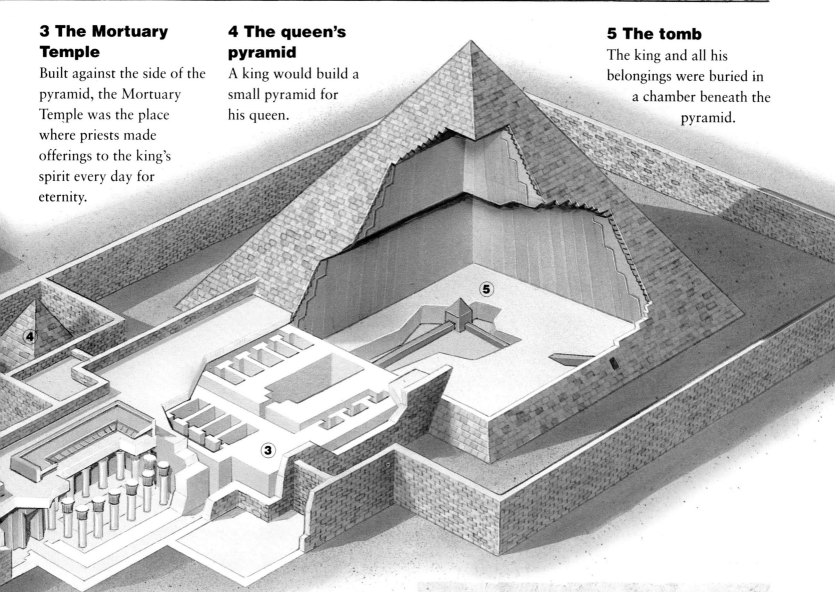

The remains of more than 20 kings' pyramids survive from the Old Kingdom. Dynasty IV pyramids are the best. Those of Dynasties V and VI were smaller and not built so well. By then, changes were taking place within Egypt. The nobles and provincial governors became rich. Trade was interrupted by trouble abroad, and so the kings gradually lost wealth and power.

Leveling the site

A low wall was built around the chosen site. The whole area was then flooded with water. Trenches were cut into the rock and measured. The bottoms of all the trenches were exactly the same depth below the surface of the water. The water was drained and the rock between the trenches cut away.

◄ Stonemasons used special rods to check that a stone block was accurately cut. The rods were held at right angles to the stone so that the string was stretched tight.

► Copper chisels and hard wooden mallets were used on limestone blocks. A plumb line made sure that the sides were straight.

▼ The blocks stayed in the quarry until the flood season, then they were loaded onto barges. Thanks to the floodwater, the barges could get close to both the quarry and the pyramid. Great skill was needed to control the heavily-laden barges on the fast-flowing river.

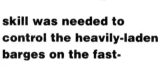

▼ Once they had been hauled up the ramp, ropes and levers were used to maneuver the huge blocks into position. An overseer checked that each block was correctly laid.

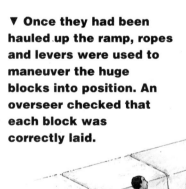

Tools of the trade

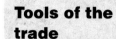

Chisels were made of copper (1) and, by the Middle Kingdom, bronze (2). Wood was used for clamps (3) and mallets (4). Dolerite pounders (5) were needed for granite blocks. Smooth stones (6) and plumb lines (7) were used to give the finish.

Work in progress

The pyramids were built mainly of limestone, which was quarried near the site. The very fine white limestone for the polished casing came from Tura, a quarry on the east bank close to where modern Cairo now stands. Some burial chambers were lined with slabs of much harder granite. This came from Aswan, farther up the Nile River.

► A pyramid-shaped capstone went on top of the pyramid. Some historians think that the Giza capstones were covered with gold.

When the pyramid reached its planned height, the casing stones were put on, beginning at the top with a pyramid-shaped capstone. The Egyptians were highly skilled at fitting and polishing the casing blocks. Those of Khufu's pyramid fitted so perfectly that you could not get a knife blade between them. Over the years most of the casing blocks have been stolen for building stone. Khafre's pyramid at Giza is the only pyramid with some left at the top.

▶ Laborers rubbed the casing blocks with polishing stones until they shone in the sun. Overseers used plumb lines to check that the angle of the slope was correct.

▼ As the men worked down the pyramid the ramp was demolished.

▶ Accidents were common on the site. Every day doctors treated broken and sprained limbs.

The final touches

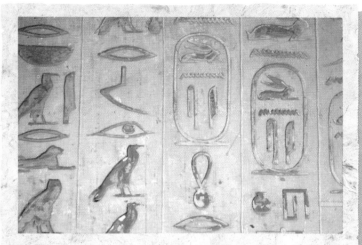

The temples and other tombs were built at the same time as the pyramid. The inside of a temple was filled with sand as the walls rose, so that blocks could be pulled straight across. When the walls and roof were finished the sand was removed. Carving and painting were done using the sand as a platform.

Pyramid Texts
Unas was the last king of Dynasty V. The walls of his burial chamber are inscribed with prayers and rituals called the Pyramid Texts. The texts are intended to help the king into the Next World and to assure his well-being there.

Columns
Stone columns supported the roofs of temples and colonnades. The tops were carved to represent lotus buds, flowering papyrus reeds, or date palms.

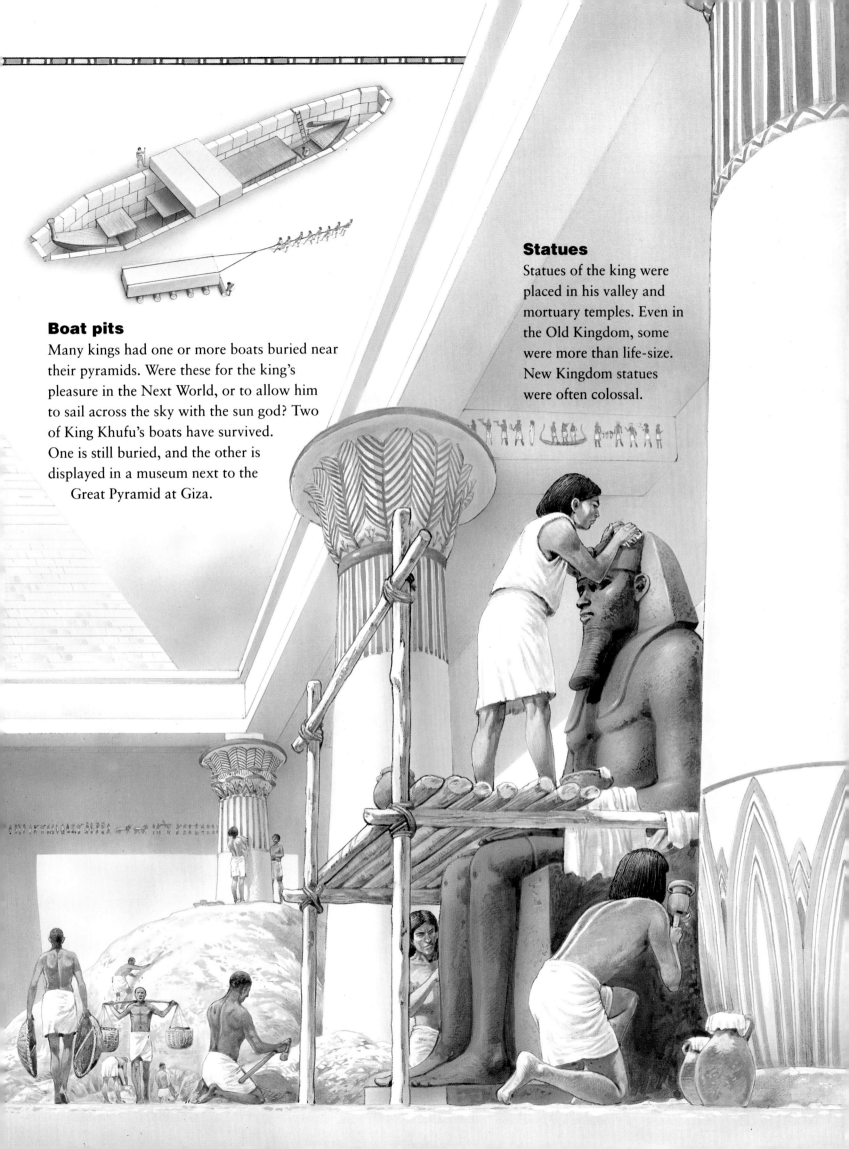

Boat pits

Many kings had one or more boats buried near their pyramids. Were these for the king's pleasure in the Next World, or to allow him to sail across the sky with the sun god? Two of King Khufu's boats have survived. One is still buried, and the other is displayed in a museum next to the Great Pyramid at Giza.

Statues

Statues of the king were placed in his valley and mortuary temples. Even in the Old Kingdom, some were more than life-size. New Kingdom statues were often colossal.

The Giza pyramids

The pyramids at Giza were built by Khufu, his son Khafre, and grandson Menkaure. Khufu's, the Great Pyramid, is the largest. It is 482 feet (147 m) tall and built with about 2,300,000 blocks. Khafre's pyramid, ten feet shorter, now looks taller because it was built on higher ground and has some of its original casing at the top. Menkaure's pyramid is the smallest, standing only 217 feet (66 m) high.

Inside the Great Pyramid

Unlike later pyramids, Khufu's has several chambers and galleries inside. Perhaps the plans were changed during construction. Khufu was buried in the top chamber.

Menkaure

Around the kings' and queens' pyramids are rows of stone mastabas for the rest of the royal family and courtiers. The site is guarded by the Sphinx, a form of the sun god. Carved from limestone, it has the body of a lion and the face of a king. The Giza pyramids are one of the wonders of the ancient world.

Khafre

The lion throne

In his Valley Temple, there were several magnificent statues of Khafre. This statue is made of diorite. The king is larger than life, sitting on a lion throne. The hawk of Horus, wings outstretched, is perched behind his head. Khafre's cartouche—his hieroglyphic name framed by an oval loop—is by his right foot.

Khufu

27

The king's covered body is taken from his palace in Memphis, across the Nile to his pyramid complex. His body will be cared for in a temporary pavilion, or kiosk, on the Valley Temple's roof.

The barge with the king's body is towed. The other ships have rowers. On the prow of one ship stand four of the king's bodyguards, carrying the royal standards.

Priests and priestesses pray for the king while his family and courtiers mourn. Other boats carry things needed for the embalming. His furniture and treasures to go in the tomb will come in the funeral procession.

A ROYAL FUNERAL

The king is dead. His people are afraid, believing that the forces of evil have gained the upper hand. His son will become king tomorrow—making a new start as a new day dawns. This will restore the balance that exists between good and evil, which the Egyptians believed was very important. Now the dead king needs the people's help urgently. His human body must be preserved and his divine spirit cared for. Prayers and rituals will guarantee the king's safe passage to the Next World and a happy eternity.

A ramp to heaven

The Egyptians liked things to have meanings. It made them seem important and magical. So a pyramid is a ramp to heaven, but it also represents a hill that was the first land. Once the whole world was covered with water, and then a hill appeared. The sun god stood on the hill to create the world. A pyramid is also the *benben*—the stone, sacred to Ra, that had fallen from heaven. All these were excellent, magic places for a spirit to go to be reborn into the Next World.

▲ The Opening of the Mouth ceremony gave life back to the mummy so that the dead person would be able to speak and move in the Next World.

▼ First the embalmers removed the brain. Then they made a slit in the left side and took out the liver, lungs, stomach, and intestines. These were preserved in a salt called natron and in resin and put into canopic jars. Each jar had the head of a guardian god.

Mummies

The Egyptians believed that if they wanted to enjoy the Next World properly their bodies had to survive. When the pyramids were built, they were still trying to find the best way to preserve dead bodies. This process is called embalming.

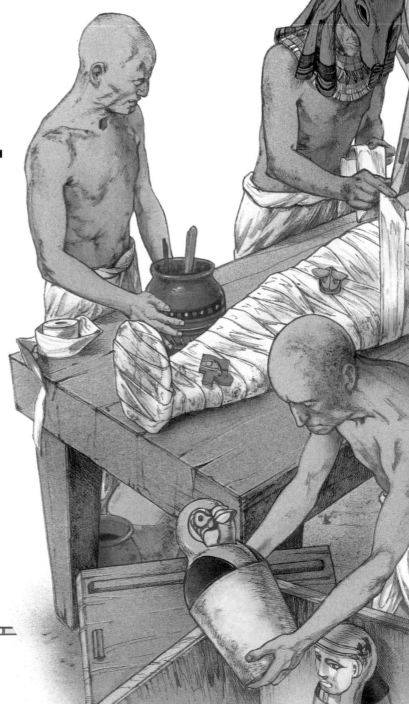

▼ The body was placed in an embalming bath and covered with natron for 40 days. This dried all the fluids out of it. The body was then washed and rubbed with oil and fragrant spices. The inside was stuffed with resin and natron, wrapped in linen. The face was painted to make it look lifelike, and the hair was neatly arranged.

By the New Kingdom, embalmers were highly skilled. It took 70 days to prepare a body. Only kings and nobles could afford the full treatment shown here. Others had to be content with a simpler process. Although most royal tombs were robbed, several mummies have survived.

Amulets

Magical amulets placed between the mummy's bandages were symbols of power, protection, and rebirth. They were intended to help the person on their journey into the Next World.

◄ **The body was wrapped in linen bandages that had been soaked in resin, so that it would hold its shape. Fingers and toes, legs and arms were first wrapped separately, then these parts were all bound together. The finished mummy was placed in a wooden coffin.**

► **Priests said prayers to help the dead person on their way through the Next World. Here the chief embalmer dressed as Anubis, god of embalming, blesses the completed mummy.**

The funeral cult

The funeral is over. The king has joined the gods, but that is not the end of the story. Estates have been set aside and priests have been appointed to provide offerings to his spirit forever, thus guaranteeing his comfort in the Next World. These cults often lasted many years, but eventually ceased—usually in one of the periods of upheaval between the Old, Middle, and New Kingdoms.

decorative jar

Tomb robbers
In the troubled times that occurred at the end of the Old, Middle, and New Kingdoms, tombs were not properly guarded and robbers broke in. All the pyramids were robbed.

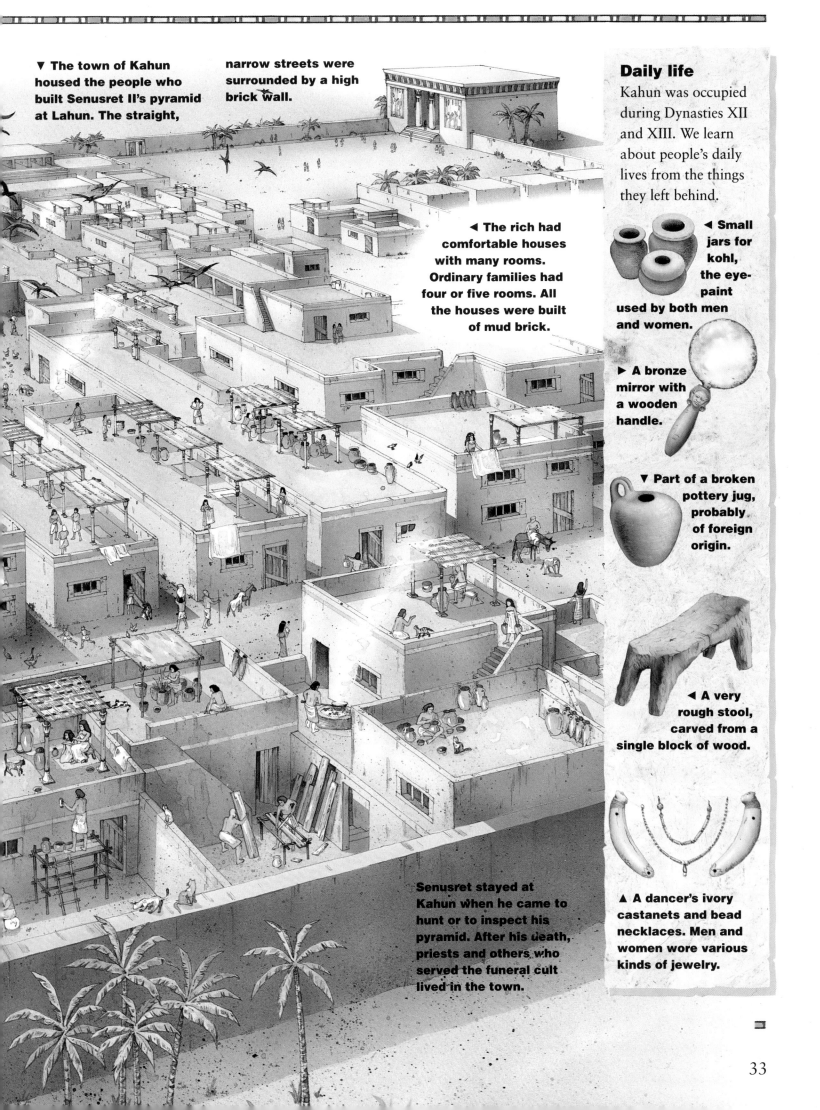

▼ The town of Kahun housed the people who built Senusret II's pyramid at Lahun. The straight, narrow streets were surrounded by a high brick wall.

◀ The rich had comfortable houses with many rooms. Ordinary families had four or five rooms. All the houses were built of mud brick.

Senusret stayed at Kahun when he came to hunt or to inspect his pyramid. After his death, priests and others who served the funeral cult lived in the town.

Daily life

Kahun was occupied during Dynasties XII and XIII. We learn about people's daily lives from the things they left behind.

◀ Small jars for kohl, the eye-paint used by both men and women.

▶ A bronze mirror with a wooden handle.

▼ Part of a broken pottery jug, probably of foreign origin.

◀ A very rough stool, carved from a single block of wood.

▲ A dancer's ivory castanets and bead necklaces. Men and women wore various kinds of jewelry.

33

The Next World

The Egyptians believed that after death they would live in the Kingdom of Osiris. They would be closer to the gods, enjoy a better life, and have greater powers than on earth. A king, who had been Horus on earth, became one with Horus's father Osiris after death. Being a god, the king had other privileges, too. As the centuries passed, ordinary people hoped to enjoy some of the comforts of the royal afterlife.

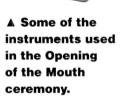

▲ Some of the instruments used in the Opening of the Mouth ceremony.

The sun god's boat

By day, dead kings could sail across the sky with Ra. At night, they accompanied him through the Underworld, bringing light to the Kingdom of Osiris. Because everyone traveled by boat in Egypt, they assumed that the sun also used one.

Ba and ka

Just as there are many sides to a person's character, so the ancient Egyptians believed they had several souls. The *ka*, the life force, stayed in the tomb, drawing strength from the food offerings. The *ka* is often shown as a pair of upraised arms. The *ba*, the personality, could go anywhere it wanted and assume any form, but it is often pictured as a human-headed bird. The *ba* represented the spirit that faced judgment in the Underworld.

The *akh* was a shining, glorified spirit that could move with the gods and the Imperishable Stars. It was shown as a crested ibis.

▲ The Book of the Dead helped the dead on their journey to the Next World. This picture is from the book of Ani.

The northern stars

A possible destination for the dead king was the stars, either those that circle the North Pole or the stars we call Orion, which the ancient Egyptians believed housed Osiris's soul.

Tomb offerings

The Egyptians expected their descendants to go on making food offerings. These were placed before a false door in the wall of the Mortuary Temple. Dead kings got daily offerings, but most people received theirs only at festivals for the dead. If the offerings stopped, the prayers and scenes on the tomb and temple walls made sure that the dead got what they needed in the Next World.

▲ The dead man and his wife are brought into the hall of judgment. The trial takes place before the god Osiris.

▲ Anubis weighs the dead person's heart against the feather of truth. A good life means a heart as light as a feather.

▲ Thoth, god of learning, acts as the scribe of the gods. He writes down the verdict of the court when it passes judgment.

▲ A sinful heart weighs more than the feather and is eaten by a monster. The virtuous pass on to an eternal life.

On the pyramid-shaped peak above the Valley of the Kings lived the goddess Meretseger, who protected the area. The Medjay, a special police force, patrolled constantly.

A royal funeral wends its way to the Valley of the Kings. In the New Kingdom Egypt was very rich. Incredible amounts of treasure were buried with the kings.

Mortuary temples were no longer built next to the tombs, but on the other side of the cliffs. The daily offerings were made there.

NEW KINGDOM TOMBS

Kings of the Old, Middle, and early New Kingdoms were buried in pyramids. The pyramids varied in size and quality, but all of them were robbed. Ineni, chief architect of King Thutmose I, designed a new style of tomb. The capital was then at Thebes, and the king was to be buried there, on the west bank of the Nile, in a tomb cut into the cliffs of a desert valley. Why did Ineni choose that particular valley? Was it because the peak that towers above it is shaped like a pyramid?

Inside a tomb

The tombs in the Valley of the Kings vary slightly in size and design. The entrance (1) was sealed for eternity. A well (2) was an obstacle to robbers and also acted as a drain during rare storms. Each tomb had halls and side chambers (3) as well as the burial chamber (4). The walls were covered with reliefs showing the progress of the sun through the Underworld. The king was reborn with the sun every day.

Pyramids for the people

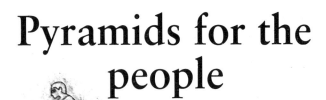

At the very time that kings stopped building pyramids, some of their subjects took over the idea. Many New Kingdom nobles were buried in ordinary rock-cut tombs on the West Bank at Thebes, but the nobles who were buried at Saqqâra, in the north, also had small pyramids as part of the design of their funeral monuments.

The tomb of Sennedjem

Sennedjem was an overseer who lived at Deir el Medina. Pictures from his tomb show him crossing the river of death. He and his wife then enjoy eternal life in a land that is like Egypt, but free of all troubles. The crops grow so well that there is never any famine, and the shady gardens are magnificent.

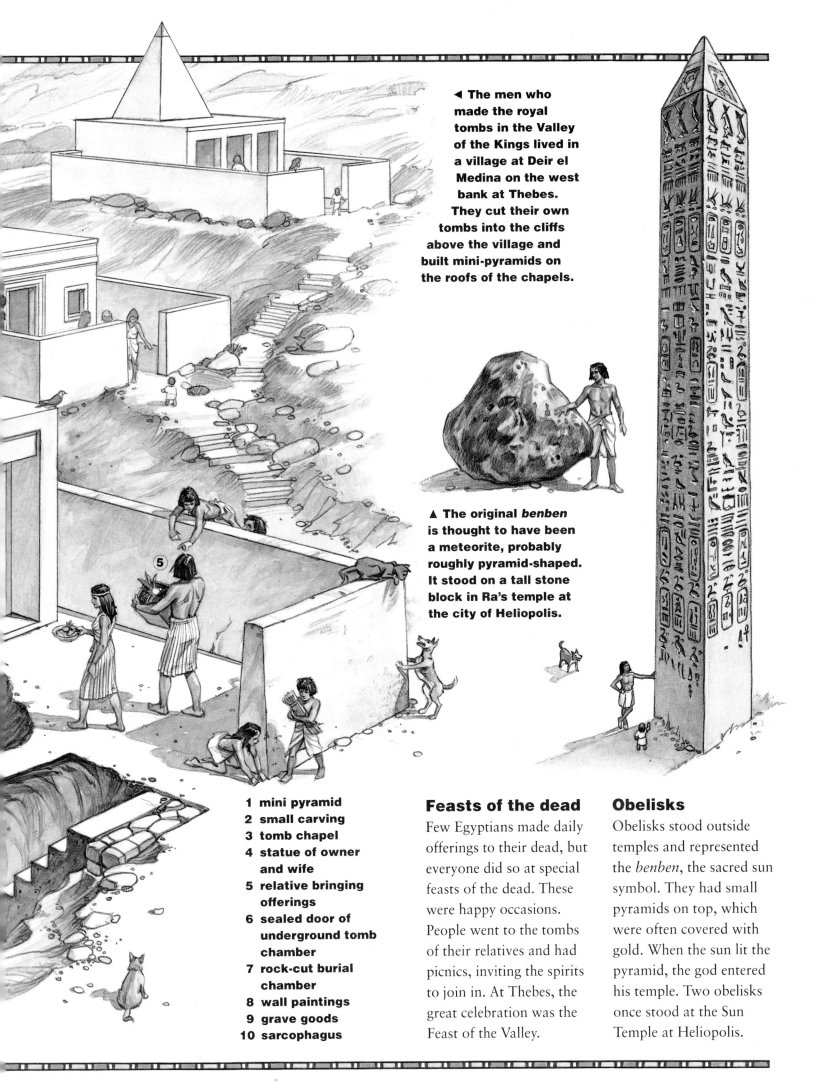

◄ The men who made the royal tombs in the Valley of the Kings lived in a village at Deir el Medina on the west bank at Thebes. They cut their own tombs into the cliffs above the village and built mini-pyramids on the roofs of the chapels.

▲ The original *benben* is thought to have been a meteorite, probably roughly pyramid-shaped. It stood on a tall stone block in Ra's temple at the city of Heliopolis.

1 mini pyramid
2 small carving
3 tomb chapel
4 statue of owner and wife
5 relative bringing offerings
6 sealed door of underground tomb chamber
7 rock-cut burial chamber
8 wall paintings
9 grave goods
10 sarcophagus

Feasts of the dead

Few Egyptians made daily offerings to their dead, but everyone did so at special feasts of the dead. These were happy occasions. People went to the tombs of their relatives and had picnics, inviting the spirits to join in. At Thebes, the great celebration was the Feast of the Valley.

Obelisks

Obelisks stood outside temples and represented the *benben*, the sacred sun symbol. They had small pyramids on top, which were often covered with gold. When the sun lit the pyramid, the god entered his temple. Two obelisks once stood at the Sun Temple at Heliopolis.

Clues to the past

Kings and commoners were buried with furniture and other goods they would need in the Next World. Egypt's dry climate has preserved them. The few tombs that have not been robbed provide information about how people lived. One of the richest is the tomb of Tutankhamen.

▶ Over a yard in length, this fan once had ostrich feathers fitted in the top.

▼ Four golden shrines fitted one within the other filled the burial chamber with only a few inches to spare.

▼ A gold portrait mask covered the king's face.

Tutankhamen's tomb

1 entrance, sealed for eternity
2 antechamber, with the king's belongings
3 Lady Evelyn Herbert, Lord Carnarvon's daughter
4 statues of the king
5 burial chamber
6 Howard Carter and Lord Carnarvon, who excavated the tomb
7 treasury
8 golden shrine, containing the king's canopic chest
9 Anubis, the jackal god

◀ **The two outer coffins were of wood, covered with gold and inlaid with semiprecious stones. The third, innermost coffin was made of solid gold with inlays.**

◀ **This relief from the king's throne is covered in gold, silver, and precious stones. It shows the king and queen.**

▼ **The tomb contained many beautiful objects made of alabaster. This graceful carving shows the royal funeral barge.**

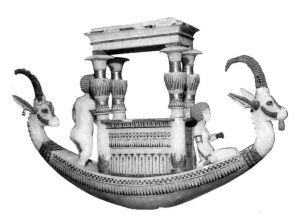

The Rosetta Stone

Because it was written in both hieroglyphs and in Greek, the Rosetta Stone provided the key to working out Egyptian picture writing. From these writings historians have been able to learn details of the religion, laws, and everyday lives of the ancient Egyptians that would otherwise be lost.

Tutankhamen

After two break-ins, Tutankhamen's tomb remained untouched until it was discovered in 1922. He is often called the Boy King because he was only about twenty when he died. His tomb was not ready, so his treasures were crammed into a smaller tomb, probably originally intended for a favored courtier.

◀ **The treasury contained many model boats intended for the king's use in the Next World.**

Hieroglyphs

The Egyptians wrote in picture signs. Some signs represent one letter; others are worth more. Vowels were supplied as the reader spoke. It takes a long time to write hieroglyphs, so a short form called hieratic was invented, followed by an even shorter form called demotic. Hieroglyphs were used until the fourth century A.D.

PYRAMIDS OF THE AMERICAS

Half a world away from Egypt, on the American continents, other people took to pyramid and mound building quite independently. It began in Central America and in the northwest of South America, but the idea soon took hold in North America.

Hopewell				Mississippians		
Maya						
Zapotecs			Toltecs		Aztecs	
Nasca	Moche		Chimú		Incas	

The Mississippian town of Etowah flourished in about A.D. 1200. Farmers, hunters, and fishermen traded their goods from the Great Lakes to the Gulf of Mexico. They used tools and weapons made of copper and stone. Temples stood on great mounds of earth, and the rulers, who adorned themselves with shells, pearls, and mica jewelry, lived on others. The whole town was protected by a wooden palisade.

The Maya

Central America was home to many peoples such as the Olmecs, Maya, Toltecs, Zapotecs, and Aztecs. The Maya, like their neighbors, built stepped pyramids. Stairways with sculptures and inscriptions led to the temples on top. Two of the best examples are the Temple of Inscriptions at Palenque and the Hieroglyphic Stairway at Copán. Occasionally, kings were buried within a pyramid.

El Mirador

El Mirador was one of the earliest Mayan cities, flourishing from about B.C. 150 to A.D. 150. It had several stepped pyramids with shrines on top. They were built of local limestone, plastered and painted red. The color red had religious importance. To sustain their gods, the Maya sacrificed their own blood by piercing their bodies with thorns. They sometimes sacrificed prisoners, too. The Maya were mathematicians and astronomers. They had a complicated system of measuring time. One of their time cycles was a year of 365 days.

▼ Archaeologists have found wall paintings at some Mayan sites. They show dramatic scenes in vivid colors. These figures come from Bonampak.

The social pyramid

The god-king (left) was at the top of the Mayan social pyramid. Nobles and warriors (center), and priests (right) formed the second rank. Next in importance were the artisans and merchants. Peasants and laborers were on the lowest step.

Craft workers

The Maya were expert stoneworkers, and they considered jade to be especially precious. Metal was not used until late in their history, and then only for jewelry, not for tools. This craft worker is carving a limestone stela with glyphs. Stelae were used to commemorate special occasions and to celebrate anniversaries.

Writing

The Maya invented a writing system that used picture signs. These hieroglyphs have only recently been decoded. Besides carving inscriptions on their monuments, the Maya also wrote books on fig-bark paper and animal skins. Only four have survived. The Spaniards, who conquered the area during the early 1500s, burned the rest.

two Mayan dates:

1 0c   **3 Cumku**   **accession**   **capture**

Chichén Itzá

The first great Mayan cities were in the southern lowlands. When the Classic Period collapsed in A.D. 900, power shifted to the north, to cities like Chichén Itzá. This city emerged from a war as the capital of a powerful state with widespread trading connections. At Chichén Itzá, Classic Mayan styles of architecture blend with those of the Toltecs, who lived in the highlands. After the collapse of Chichén Itzá, power shifted to the city of Mayapán.

▼ The Castillo, Chichén Itzá's main pyramid, was rebuilt over an earlier one. The present pyramid was built shortly before A.D. 1100. The one underneath was constructed 100 years earlier. Inside the original pyramid there was a stone sculpture of a jaguar, painted red with jade inlays for spots.

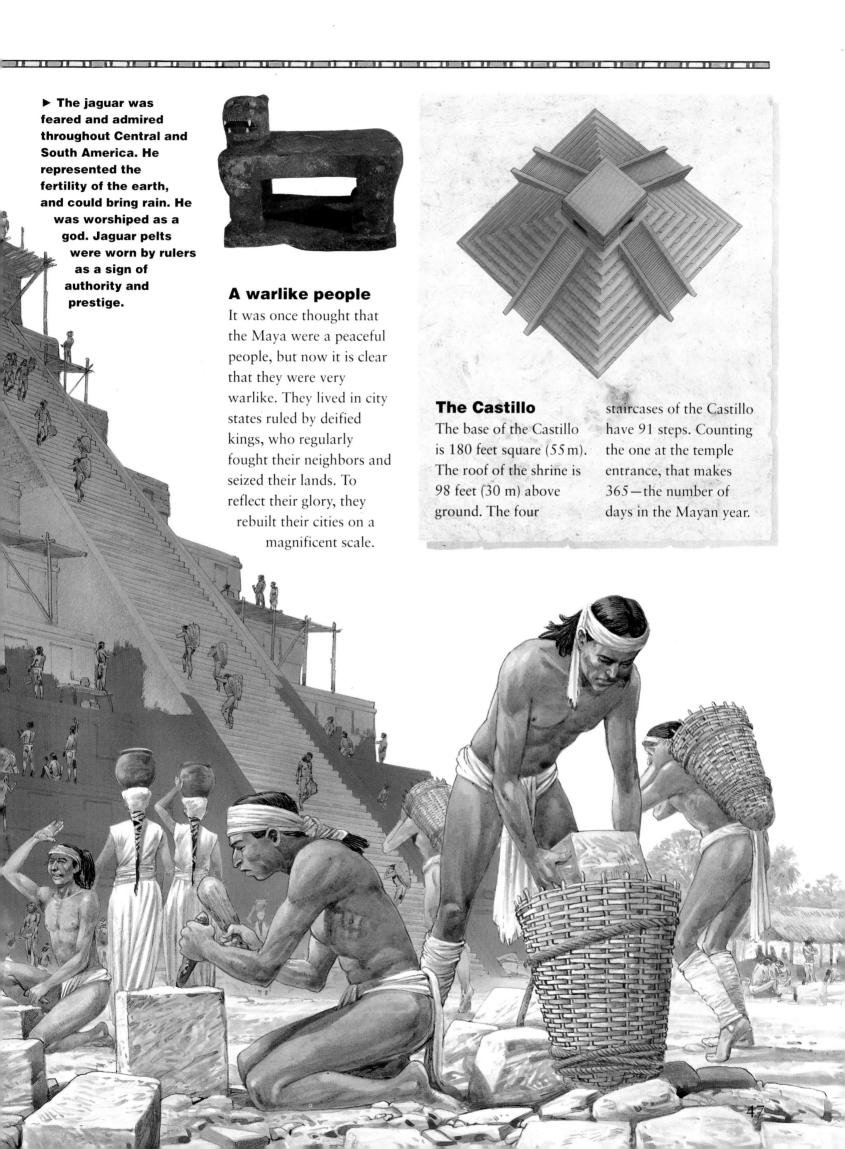

► The jaguar was feared and admired throughout Central and South America. He represented the fertility of the earth, and could bring rain. He was worshiped as a god. Jaguar pelts were worn by rulers as a sign of authority and prestige.

A warlike people

It was once thought that the Maya were a peaceful people, but now it is clear that they were very warlike. They lived in city states ruled by deified kings, who regularly fought their neighbors and seized their lands. To reflect their glory, they rebuilt their cities on a magnificent scale.

The Castillo

The base of the Castillo is 180 feet square (55 m). The roof of the shrine is 98 feet (30 m) above ground. The four staircases of the Castillo have 91 steps. Counting the one at the temple entrance, that makes 365—the number of days in the Mayan year.

The floating city

In about A.D. 1200 a tribe of hunters and farmers arrived in the Valley of Mexico looking for a place to settle. On a marshy island in Lake Texcoco they saw an eagle perched on a cactus. Believing this to be a good omen, they chose the island as the site of their capital city, Tenochtitlán. Through their skill in war, the Aztecs became rich and powerful.

3 The central precinct

The city was divided into four sectors. The Teopan quarter contained the Royal Palace and the Great Temple.

1 The Great Pyramid Temple

At the Great Pyramid Temple sacrifices were made to the gods.

2 Canals

Canals connected all the different parts of the city. The Aztecs used them as roads, traveling around in small, flat-bottomed boats. There were sidewalks for walking along each side of the canals.

4 Causeways

Causeways connected Tenochtitlán to the mainland. They were wide enough for three horses to ride side by side.

5 Suburbs

The Aztecs also began to spread to other islands and to build on them.

6 The aqueduct

Fresh water was brought from the mainland in a covered aqueduct.

⑥

7 Chinampas

As the population of the city increased, the Aztecs made more space for themselves by making floating gardens called chinampas.

⑦

Farming the land

Corn was the main crop for all the peoples of Central America. It was the New World equivalent of wheat, barley, or rice. The Aztecs also grew many fruits and vegetables on their fertile chinampas. Special harvest festivals were celebrated to thank the gods and goddesses for their bounty. They kept turkeys and small, hairless dogs for meat and hunted deer, rabbits, and wild pigs. The lake provided them with fish and waterfowl.

sweet potatoes

avocados

corn

squash

chilies

tomatoes

▶ Every man helped to make new chinampas for his family.

◀ Bundles of reeds were woven into a floating platform. Then willow posts were hammered in around the edge.

▼ Rich black mud was dredged from the bottom of the lake. This was spread on top of the reed platform and left to harden. The chinampas were very fertile, but needed a lot of care.

▶ The roots of trees planted around the edge helped to anchor the soil and stop it from falling back into the lake.

Tenochtitlán became a bustling city with around 300,000 inhabitants. It was much larger than any other town in the world at that time. In 1520, the Spanish conquerors were impressed by Tenochtitlán's beauty and cleanliness.

The Great Pyramid Temple

The Aztecs believed that the sun god needed blood from human hearts to strengthen him. Without blood, the sun would die and the world come to an end. So human sacrifices were essential. The Great Pyramid Temple was the main religious building in Tenochtitlán.

The Aztecs were a warlike people. All the boys were trained to be warriors, and prisoners were destined for sacrifice.

The warriors who captured the most prisoners became wealthy and powerful.

feather shield

Those who failed to capture any prisoners were disgraced. Conquered peoples were forced to pay tribute to the Aztec emperor. Most soldiers returned after a war to work as farmers, artisans, or merchants.

Seven temples

The great stepped pyramid was at the center of the sacred enclosure in Tenochtitlán. On top were the twin shrines dedicated to Huitzilopochtli, god of the sun and war, and Tlaloc, the rain god. It was here that the Aztecs carried out their most terrible ceremonies involving human sacrifice. Priests killed their victims on the altar at the top of the pyramid. Six earlier pyramids have been found under the one destroyed by the Spaniards. Each new temple was more magnificent than the temple it replaced.

Warriors and priests

The eagle and jaguar knights, who were the leading warriors, were drawn from the noble class. So, too, were the priests. Some artisans were held in high esteem, particularly those who worked with gold or feathers. Merchants had power, but lacked prestige. Unskilled workers made up the lowest class.

The Moche

In the northwest of South America, other great cultures also built flat-topped, stepped pyramids and mounds. These peoples included the Chavín, Nasca, Moche, Chimú, and Incas. The Moche lived along the northern coast of what is now Peru. They built an excellent irrigation system that made use of all their land. The fields were kept fertile by spreading them with the droppings of seabirds, called guano, which is an excellent fertilizer.

▲ To make sun-dried mud bricks, earth, water, and chopped straw were put in shallow pits, and then people trampled all the materials together. The straw helped to strengthen and bind the mud.

▲ The mud is shaped into bricks in a wooden mold that has no top or bottom, so that it can be used again. The bricks dry rock-hard in the sun.

▲ The Moche were outstanding potters. Their most elaborate pots represent the people and animals around them. They tell us a lot about daily life and what the people looked like.

The Nasca

The Nasca lived in southern Peru. Their weavers produced brightly-colored, patterned textiles. However, they are best remembered for their mysterious "lines" — the huge pictures of birds and animals that were outlined on the desert.

The Moche were farmers, fishermen, and traders. They never invented a writing system, but they were great artisans and builders. Their buildings were made of adobe, sun-dried mud bricks. This kind of brick is used throughout the world, where the climate is suitable. The largest Moche pyramid was the Pyramid of the Sun. It was 135 feet (41 m) tall and contained over 143 million bricks. The Pyramid of the Moon was built of over 50 million bricks.

► The Moche were skilled workers of copper, silver, and gold. This tiny figure of a warrior-lord, made of gold, silver, and turquoise, was a nose ornament. It was found during the excavation of a tomb near Sipán.

The Sipán pyramid
Before a ceremony a Moche ruler was decked out in all his finery. We know about the costume and jewelry from items buried with rulers of Sipán. Two of their burials were found under a platform near the Sipán pyramid.

◄ The bricks are strong and under normal conditions last for many centuries. However, during the 1600s, Spanish treasure-hunters diverted a river to wash away the Pyramid of the Sun so that they could search for gold that lay beneath.

The Incas

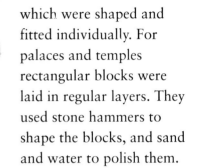

The Incas flourished in the northwest of South America from 1438 to 1532. Their rulers, the Sapa Incas, were thought to be direct descendants of the sun. They alone could marry their sisters. Nobles of royal blood and others who were allowed the same privileges formed the highest nobility. Under them were lesser nobles, who were local officials, and then came the commoners. In Inca society everyone had to work and make a contribution to the community, in line with their rank and talents. Those in need were cared for by the government.

Building walls

The Incas were expert stonemasons. For walls and terraces they used large many-sided blocks, which were shaped and fitted individually. For palaces and temples rectangular blocks were laid in regular layers. They used stone hammers to shape the blocks, and sand and water to polish them.

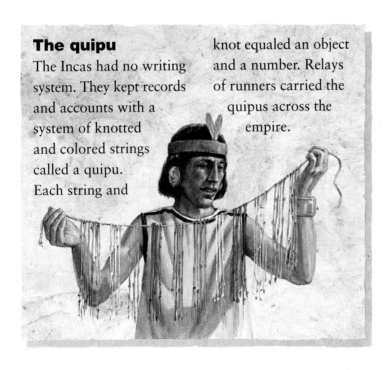

The quipu

The Incas had no writing system. They kept records and accounts with a system of knotted and colored strings called a quipu. Each string and knot equaled an object and a number. Relays of runners carried the quipus across the empire.

Through the deserts, mountains, and jungles of their homeland the Incas built excellent roads. Much of the farmland was in the Andes mountains, so they carved flat terraces on the slopes to allow them to grow corn and potatoes. They also mined vast quantities of copper, gold, and silver.

Temple of the Sun
The Temple of the Sun was built on a terraced platform and dominated the southeastern corner of the capital city, Cuzco. It was the holiest shrine in the empire. Here, in a temple with a golden frieze around the walls, there was an enormous gold disk, which represented the sun god, ancestor of the Inca emperors. In the courtyard there were gold statues of plants and llamas.

Pyramids around the world

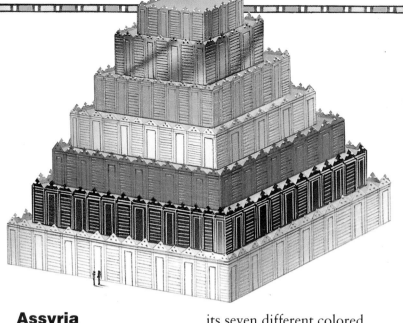

Other cultures have also incorporated the pyramid form into their building designs, but most were not intended for tombs. The peoples of ancient Mesopotamia, the land between the rivers Tigris and Euphrates that is now modern Iraq, were enthusiastic builders of stepped platforms. However, there was a shortage of stone and good timber, so they built them with mud brick.

Sumer

The Sumerians, the first inhabitants of southern Mesopotamia, built temples on low platforms. When new temples were required, they were built on top of the remains of the old, so the platforms beneath got taller. Liking the effect, the Sumerians built all new temples on ziggurats, or temple platforms. The shrines on top became insignificant compared to the huge ziggurats. The platforms were so large they had to be terraced, forming a sort of step pyramid. This one was built in the city of Ur in about 2000 B.C.

Assyria

The Assyrians lived in northern Mesopotamia. They began conquering their great empire during the 700s B.C. and dominated the area until 614 B.C. Like their neighbors, the Assyrians built great ziggurats to honor their gods. This spectacular ziggurat with its seven different colored steps was at Khorsabad. It was over 130 feet (40 m) tall. Khorsabad was built by King Sargon II (721–701 B.C.) as a grand new capital for his empire, but he died shortly after it was completed. The city was then abandoned and fell into ruins.

Nubia

At the end of Egypt's New Kingdom, Nubia gained independence and was ruled by kings of its own. Much of the culture and religion was of Egyptian origin. The kings adopted old-style Egyptian burials, erecting pyramid tombs for themselves and their families at El Kurru and Nuri. The pyramids were built of local sandstone and had steep sides. The burial chambers were cut into the rock below, and some were decorated with Egyptian-style scenes.

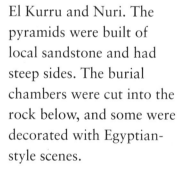

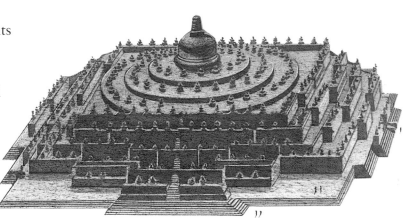

Babylon

The Babylonians rose to power in Mesopotamia around 2000 B.C. They took over the old Sumerian ideas and built ziggurats. This is the Etemenanki, Babylon's great ziggurat. It was rebuilt during the New Empire (625–539 B.C.) on a scale fitting for the capital of their new, vast empire.

Perhaps 200,000 inhabitants thronged Babylon in its heyday. The ziggurat was about 330 feet (100 m) tall and may have inspired the Biblical story of the Tower of Babel.

Java

It took over a million blocks of local stone to build Borobudur in Java. The base is 370 feet square (113 m), with five steps above. On top of these are three circular terraces, on which are 72 stupas containing statues of Buddha. In the center there is a huge stupa. The different levels reflect ideas in the Buddhist faith. The temple symbolizes the universe, and also a mountain, a sacred place in Southeast Asia. It can help worshipers to meditate, and it is a center for religious rituals.

Rome

Many people have been impressed by ancient Egypt, its monuments and long history. The Romans were also much impressed by Egyptian piety. The cult of the goddess Isis spread across the Roman Empire as far as Hadrian's Wall in Britain! Such interest may explain why a pyramid funeral monument was built at Rome. In Victorian times, Egypt was once again fascinating to Europeans. Tours took increasing numbers of people to gaze at the wonders of the pharaohs. When they got home, some chose to have stone monuments built over their graves in the shape of pyramids.

Myanmar (Burma)

Dhammayangyi is one of several Buddhist temples at Pagan in Myanmar. King Narathu (1169–74) killed his father, brother, and wife. He built the temple to atone for his sins, but killed the architect so that he could not build another one like it. The temple is square, built around a central pillar. The kiln-fired brickwork is very fine—perhaps because Narathu cut off the hands of any bricklayer whose work was not perfect!

Pyramid power

Pyramids have been studied by archaeologists for over a hundred years, and we are still finding out things about them. They have also inspired a whole series of strange theories and weird ideas. Modern advertisers have recognized the fascination and power of pyramids and use pictures of them to sell many products.

▲ In 1993 this tiny robot explored a small shaft in the Great Pyramid at Giza and found a sealed opening at the end.

Transamerica pyramid

Many modern architects outside of Egypt have taken the pyramid form and adapted it. Using modern materials like glass and steel, they have produced some fantastic variations. In San Francisco, the Transamerica pyramid dominates the skyline. The pyramid shape is part of a design to withstand the frequent earthquakes that occur in the area. The pyramid was built in 1970. The tip is 853 feet (260 m) high.

A new pyramid after 3,000 years!

This elegant modern version of a pyramid is a monument to the memory of Egypt's President Sadat and to the Unknown Warrior. The sides are completely covered with texts from the Koran.

Theories about pyramids

In the Middle Ages some people thought that pyramids were Joseph's granaries. A story in the Bible tells how Joseph predicted famine in Egypt, and suggested to the pharaoh that they should store grain in granaries. Other people believed that the pyramids were places where priests observed the stars. In Victorian times people believed the Great Pyramid was divinely inspired and could be used to predict the future. Some modern theorists claim that visitors from other planets were involved in the building of the Giza pyramids!

Star connection

Research has shown that two of the narrow shafts in the Great Pyramid point to the polar stars. A third points to Orion, and a fourth to Sirius.

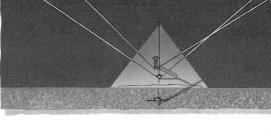

Canary Wharf Tower

Among many eye-catching modern buildings is the 50-story skyscraper at Canary Wharf in the developing area of London's Docklands. With its pillar-like tower, supporting a pyramid, it resembles a gigantic obelisk. It is the tallest building in Great Britain.

Louvre pyramid

The sides of the glass pyramid built as an entrance to the Louvre in Paris rise at the same angle as the Great Pyramid. Some people feel that the pyramid does not blend in with the great Renaissance palace.

Glossary

adobe The name given in Central and South America to sun-dried mud bricks.

adze A tool with a curved blade, often used for scraping.

afterlife Life after death.

amulet A charm worn to bring good luck or to protect someone from harm.

archaeologist A person who studies ancient peoples by digging up their tools and the remains of buildings.

architect A person who designs buildings.

astronomy The scientific study of the stars and planets.

barracks Large plain building where a number of soldiers or workers live.

Book of the Dead This was written on a papyrus scroll and placed in or near the coffin. Based on the Pyramid Texts, but intended for use by commoners as well as royalty, it tells the dead person how to overcome all dangers and successfully reach the Kingdom of Osiris.

canopic jars Jars in which an Egyptian mummy's internal organs were stored. In the Middle Kingdom the lids had human heads; by the New Kingdom they were made in the form of the heads of the four sons of Horus—man, baboon, jackal, and hawk.

capstone The topmost stone of a pyramid, itself pyramid-shaped.

CANOPIC JARS

baboon   man   hawk   jackal

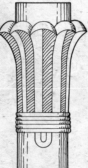

CARTOUCHE

cartouche An oval frame drawn around the name of a king or queen. It comes from the hieroglyphic sign for protection.

casing stones The outermost layer of a pyramid, covering all the stones inside.

chinampas The artificial islands in Lake Texcoco, made by the Aztecs from wood, reeds, and mud. They were used to grow vegetables and fruit.

chisel Tool with a straight, sharp blade used to shape wood or stone.

column A tall pillar used for supporting roofs, decorated with carvings of papyrus or palm leaves.

COLUMNS

crook A short stick, curved at the top like a shepherd's crook, which was part of ancient Egypt's royal regalia.

palm

cult Religious worship, or the special rituals used in worship.

diorite A very hard stone, mottled black and white, used for making statues.

dikes High earth banks, often with a ditch on one side, built to protect villages or land from floodwaters.

dynasty A line of rulers, members of the same family who inherit the throne, one from another.

embalm To preserve a body from decay.

flail A handle with three strings of beads which was part of ancient Egypt's royal regalia.

frieze A band of decoration running along the top of a wall.

granite A very hard stone, found around the modern town of

Aswan in Egypt. It can be pink or gray in color, with shiny crystal specks.

grave goods The items placed in a grave for the dead person's use or enjoyment in the Next World.

guano Name used in South America to describe the droppings of the millions of seabirds that nest along the west coast.

bundle papyrus

heb sed The Feast of the Tail—an ancient Egyptian ceremony, usually held when a king had reigned for thirty years, to renew his strength. It is named after the day the king first put on the bull's tail, which is part of the royal regalia.

hieroglyphs Picture writing.

jade A hard green stone.

open papyrus

jaguar A large member of the cat family with a spotted coat. It is found in Central and South America and is a deadly hunter.

kiosk A lightweight structure, usually with a back and two sides. A pavilion.

kohl A dark paint, used to outline the eyes.

limestone A white stone which is easy to cut and carve. The Egyptian pyramids were built of limestone blocks.

llama A South American animal, kept for its fine wool and as a beast of burden.

mallet A hammer, usually made of wood.

mastaba An Arabic word meaning a mud-brick bench. This modern name was given to some ancient Egyptian tombs at Giza and Saqqâra because they had the same shape.

meteorite Fragment of rock or metal that has fallen to earth from space.

Mortuary Temple In an ancient Egyptian pyramid complex, this was the place where daily offerings were made to the king's spirit.

mummy An embalmed body. The word comes from the Arabic *mumiya*, meaning pitch. Some mummies had turned black, so it was thought they had been covered in pitch.

natron A natural salt. The Egyptians mined it in the Wadi el Natrun.

Next World The place a person's soul went to live after he or she died.

MUMMY

obelisk A tall square stone pillar with a pyramid-shaped top.

offerings Gifts of food, drink, and so on that were made to dead relatives or to dead royalty.

Opening of the Mouth An important part of the ancient Egyptian burial service. The rite involves touching the mummy with a ceremonial adze to open the mouth and give back the powers of speech and movement.

palette A wood or stone slab used for mixing paints or ink.

palisade A wall made of strong pointed wooden stakes, often used to defend a town.

papyrus A reed. The Egyptians sliced the stem into strips and pressed them together to make a kind of paper.

pharaoh The name comes from two ancient Egyptian words: *per 'o*, meaning Great House, or palace. It referred to the king, as we might say "the White House announced ..." to refer to the President.

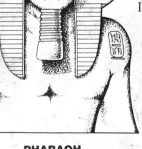

PHARAOH

plumb line String with a weight on the end, used to check that a stone or whole wall is absolutely straight.

polar stars The group of stars that revolves above the North Pole. The Egyptians called them the Imperishable Ones, because they never set below the horizon.

SAPA INCA

quipu An ancient Inca way of keeping records, made of a series of colored strings with knots.

ramp A slope that joins the ground to a higher level.

regalia The crowns, scepters, and other ceremonial items worn by a king or queen to show their rank.

relief A carved picture that decorates a wall.

resin A sticky substance that comes from the stems or trunks of some plants and trees.

sacrifice Something that is given as an offering to a god, such as food, wine, incense, flowers, or even animal or human life.

Sapa Inca The supreme Inca, who held a position similar to that of an emperor.

sarcophagus The outer coffin, made of stone, in which a wooden coffin was laid.

scribe In ancient times, a person who could write.

He copied documents and wrote letters for a living.

PLUMB LINE

shrine A place that contains a statue of a god or a holy relic.

sledge A pair of runners joined together, used to pull heavy loads over sand. A heavy sled.

sphinx A form of the ancient Egyptian sun god. It had the body of a lion and the head of the reigning king or a ram. The Giza Sphinx has the face of King Khafre.

stela An upright slab of stone with inscriptions and sometimes pictures carved on it.

stupa A Buddhist monument containing a relic or statue of the Buddha.

terrace A raised, level space used for walking, standing, or growing crops.

tribute A payment made by conquered peoples to their conqueror.

tomb A grave with an elaborate building over it, or a number of rooms cut into the rock.

Valley Temple Part of an Egyptian pyramid complex, usually built where

VALLEY TEMPLE

the desert and the fields meet. A dead king's body was taken there to be prepared for burial.

yoke A wooden pole placed across a person's shoulders. Objects to be carried are hung on each end.

ziggurat The name given to the stepped temple platforms built in ancient Mesopotamia.

Index

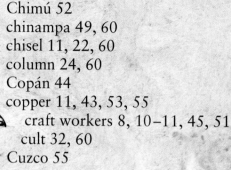

Myanmar 57

N

Nasca 52
natron 30, 61
New Kingdom 4, 12, 25, 31, 32, 37, 38
Next World 5, 6, 9, 24, 25, 29, 30, 31, 32, 34–35, 40, 53
Nile River 5, 7, 12, 13, 20
Nubia 56
Nuri 56

O

obelisk 39, 61
offering 35, 37, 38, 61
Old Kingdom 4, 8, 21, 25, 32, 37
Olmecs 44
Opening of the Mouth 29, 34, 61
Orion 59
Osiris 15, 34, 35

P

Pacal, King 44
Pagan 57
palette 11, 61
papyrus 11, 61
pharaoh 8, 61
plumb line 22, 23, 61
pottery 52
priest 8, 14, 15, 28, 31, 32, 44, 50
Ptah 14
Pyramid Texts 20, 24

Q

quarry 10, 11, 12, 22
queen's pyramid 21

quipu 54, 61

R

Ra 6, 15, 20, 29, 34, 39
ramp 17, 20, 22, 24
relief 41, 61
regalia 6, 61
robber 32, 37, 40
robot 58
Rome 57
Rosetta Stone 41

S

sacrifice 44, 50, 61
Sadat pyramid 58
Saqqâra 17, 39
Sargon II, King 56
scribe 10, 11, 61
sculptor 10
Sennedjem 39
Senusret II, King 32
ship 12
shrine 44, 47, 51, 55, 56, 61
silver 53, 55
Sipán 53
sledge 13, 17, 20, 61
Sneferu, King 19
sphinx, 27
star 15, 34, 59
statue 25
stela 45, 61
step pyramid 17, 18–19, 44–45, 52
stepped platform 56
stone 10, 11, 12, 20, 22, 54
stonemason 10, 16, 54
stupa 57, 61
straight-sided pyramid 17, 20–21
Sumeria 56

T

Temple of the Sun 55
temples 24, 39, 43, 44, 56
Tenochtitlán 48, 50
Texcoco, Lake 48
Thebes 37, 38
Thoth 35
Thutmose I, King 37
Tlaloc 51
Toltecs 44, 46

tomb 6, 18, 21, 24, 31, 36–37, 40, 61
tool 11, 22, 43, 45
Tower of Babel 57
trade 12, 21
Transamerica pyramid 58
trench 21
Turah 22
Tutankhamen 40–41

U

Unas, King 20, 24
Underworld 34, 37

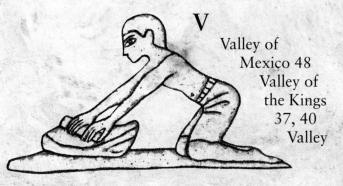

V

Valley of Mexico 48
Valley of the Kings 37, 40
Valley Temple 20, 25, 28, 61

W

wall painting 38, 39
warrior 44, 51
weapon 11, 43
weaving 52
Western Desert 7
work tax 9, 16
worship 14, 47
writing 11, 41, 45, 53

Y

yoke 12, 61

Z

Zapotecs 44
ziggurat 56, 57, 61
zodiac 15
Zoser, King 17, 18, 19

Acknowledgments

The publishers would like to thank the following
illustrators for their contribution to this book:

Julian Baker 17*r*, 18–19*t*, 19*r*, 20*t*, 20–21*c*, 22*bl*, 26*t*,
31*tr*, 49*tr*, 51*tr*; **Vanessa Card** 8, 14–15*b*, 26-7 (cartouches),
34*bl/tr*, 40*br*, 44*bl*, 45*tr*; **Peter Dennis** (Linda Rogers
Associates) 4–5, 6–7*tc/b*, 16–17, 18–19*b*, 24–25*b*, 46–47;
Francesca D'Ottavi 9, 10, 30–31*c*, 50–51;
Terry Gabbey (Associated Freelance Artists Ltd.) 38–39, 42–43;
Christa Hook (Linden Artists) 32*bl*, 35*tr*, 44*tl*, 49*c/br*, 54*tr/bl*;
Christian Hook 53*cr*; **John James** (Temple Rogers Artists
Agency) 48; **Eddy Kräherbühl** 22*t/c/br*, 23, 40–1*c*, 55;
Angus McBride 44–45*br*, 53–53*c*; **Nicki Palin** 11*r*, 12*bl*, 36–37;
Richard Ward 5*tr*, 7*tr/c*, 12*c*, 20*c*, 21*br*, 24*tl*, 32*c*,
33*r*, 34*c*, 35*tl*, 37*br*, 43*tr*, 47*tr*, 51*tl*, 52*bl/br*, 53*tr*;
Studio Boni Galante (Virgil Pomfret Agency) 26–27*c*, 32–33*c*;
Ian Thompson 56–57, 58*cl/br*, 59*tr/b*; **Shirley Tourret**
(B.L. Kearley Ltd.) 30*tl/bl*, 31*br*; **Andrew Wheatcroft**
(Virgil Pomfret Agency) 12–13, 14*t*, 15*t*, 28–29;

Page symbols by Vanessa Card
Border by John Lobban (B.L. Kearley Ltd.)

The publishers would also like to thank the following
for supplying photographs for this book:

Page 6 ZEFA
15 & 19*t* Ancient Art & Architecture Collection
19*b*, & 24 Peter Clayton
27 G. Dagli Orti
29 & 35 Michael Holford
38 Peter Clayton
40 ZEFA
41*tl* & 41*tc* ZEFA; 41*cr* British Museum
47 G. Dagli Orti
58 Anne Millard
58–59 Ancient Art & Architecture Collection
59 ZEFA